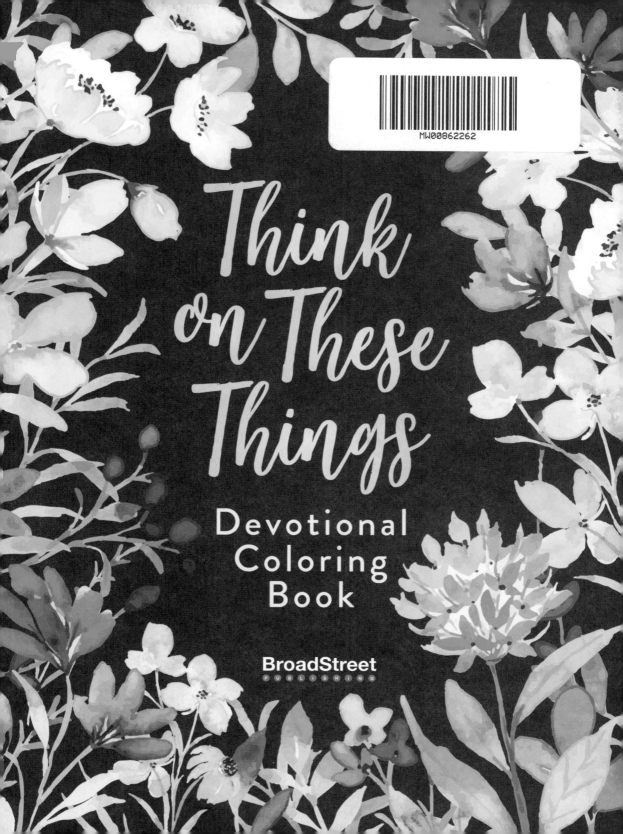

Think on These Things

Devotional Coloring Book

BroadStreet
PUBLISHING

BroadStreet Publishing®
Savage, Minnesota, USA
Majestic Expressions is an imprint of BroadStreet Publishing Group, LLC.
Broadstreetpublishing.com

Think on These Things (Devotional Coloring Book)
© 2024 BroadStreet Publishing

9781424569250

Typesetting and design by Garborg Design Works | garborgdesign.com
Compiled and edited by Michelle Winger | literallyprecise.com

Printed in China.

24   25   26   27   28   29   30   7   6   5   4   3   2   1

Introduction

Life is full of demands. Appointments, deadlines, obligations, and constant digital chatter occupy every moment and build a mountain of unhealthy stress and tension. Coloring is an effective stress reducer, but true rest and peace are found in God. He encourages us in his Word to think about things that are good, lovely, and pure.

Think on These Things perfectly combines encouraging devotions and inspiring illustrations in one beautiful book. When you choose to focus on things you are grateful for, you will find your satisfaction in life increases. Comparisons cease. Unnecessary pursuits pause. And you begin to notice the things that matter. Life. Breath. Connection. Kindness. Beauty.

Spend time reflecting on the character of God and be filled with his joy and peace. Express your creativity freely as you fill the intricate images with the beauty of color. The worries of life can wait.

All About God

From him and through him and for him are all things.
To him be the glory forever. Amen!

ROMANS 11:36 NIV

"She is very religious; she's always talking about God!" What was meant as an insult was really quite a compliment. Has this ever been said about you? Maybe it has, and it has shut you up. With cheeks flushed, you felt judged and misread by the person you were with. Do not be ashamed. What some meant as harm is really a reflection of the gift God has given you. If you have tunnel vision for Jesus, you are not on the wrong path. The Bible, and this verse in Romans, makes it pretty clear that we are to be all about the kingdom of God!

We are not called to live in a divide of the sacred and the secular, but in all things give God the glory. Not everyone will understand why you choose to make God your priority and bring him up in areas they don't think he belongs. Don't mind them. You are not too much; God loves how you can see him in all the details of life. A heart set on seeking him is exactly where it needs to be.

Well done! God is pleased and delighted in you. To be a person who sees him at work and brings attention to it is exactly what this world needs. You have a mind set on the Spirit. That is to be commended.

Jesus, my mind is set on you. My heart longs for more of you. I see you working in the world around me; thank you! Help me to never be ashamed of the gifts you have given me.

From him
and
through him
and
for him
are
all things.

Romans 11:36 NIV

Beyond the Pain

This light momentary affliction is preparing for us an eternal weight of glory beyond all comparison, as we look not to the things that are seen but to the things that are unseen. For the things that are seen are transient, but the things that are unseen are eternal.

2 Corinthians 4:17-18 esv

Light and momentary? These troubles feel anything but that! you might be thinking. This verse was written by a man who had been in prison, shipwrecked, beaten, starved, robbed, stoned, whipped, and more. If there was someone who knew about affliction, Paul could for sure qualify as an expert!

The unseen, eternal glory that is to come is unimaginably good. Incomprehensibly splendid. And on top of that, it's solid. It's not going anywhere. It's more real than any reality you've experienced. It's designed by a good Father who loves you deeply. When things feel hopeless, maybe your hope is in the wrong place. Turn your hope to the unshakeable age that is to come, to your eternal glory with Jesus Christ. That is a sustaining hope that will not disappoint and will afford you much joy in the here and now.

Remembering that your time on earth is the journey and not the destination, and that your eternal home awaits you, will help you keep your priorities aligned with Jesus.

God, help me to keep an eternal perspective when it comes to the troubles I face in this life. What is coming in the future is far better than I could ever imagine.

Called His Own

For the sake of his great name the LORD will not reject his people, because the LORD was pleased to make you his own.

1 SAMUEL 12:22 NIV

The Israelites have an extensive history, laid out for us in the Old Testament. It is often seen as back and forth: the Israelites disobeying God and God consistently redeeming them to himself. If you can think of it, it's been done by this group of people God called his own—idolatry, complaining, disobedience, murder, lying, sexual immorality, the list goes on over thousands of years. It makes you wonder if they would ever get it right, or if God would ever give up on his people. The answer to both of those is no; they would never get it right, and God would never give up.

If you find yourself shaking your head at all their shortcomings, it is wise to remember you are never going to get it right either. The good news is you don't have to! You can be secure in Jesus, no matter how right or wrong you get it. Faith in him means you are called his own.

People usually swing one of two ways, either trying to work harder for their salvation or giving up completely and accepting the title of unforgivable. The truth is that none of us have to work harder, and none of us are unforgivable. The grace of God is perfect. This status of being God's own is a free gift, and it comes with the richest of rewards.

God thank you for your grace. Thank you for calling me your own.

Empowered to Hope

May God, the inspiration and fountain of hope, fill you to overflowing with uncontainable joy and perfect peace as you trust in him. And may the power of the Holy Spirit continually surround your life with his super-abundance until you radiate with hope!

ROMANS 15:13 TPT

Think of yourself as a glass. God pours joy and peace into you. When he does that, you overflow with hope. That overflow is noticeable to everyone around you. They, in turn, acknowledge God, and it spurs them on to believe in him! The cycle starts again in a new believer. This is discipleship made simple.

When you exercise your faith muscle, spending time with Jesus, walking in obedience to him, and reading his Word, God fills you with joy and peace. This joy and peace mixed together release hope. Try and bottle it up, but why would you want to? It's a mixture waiting to be shared with others. Won't you be a vessel for his glory and overflow today?

God is not limited by your ability to be productive. He is not prone to measure your days how you measure them. The good, lasting, worthwhile work that he is doing, the glorious fruit that he produces in a person's life, comes from the Holy Spirit! Stop striving and wearing yourself out trying to achieve things for God. Let him do the work for you; partner with him to see him move.

God, please fill me with joy and peace in this moment. Let me overflow with your hope. Fill me with your power, show me your love, and let it be contagious to others.

Listen in the Dark

"What I tell you in the dark, say in the light,
and what you hear whispered, proclaim on the housetops."

MATTHEW 10:27 ESV

It is commonplace for us to create a dichotomy in our heads that says God is light, so if there is darkness, God isn't in it. That is understandable, considering all the verses we read that describe Christ as light. However, it's not true. In the psalms, we are told there is no place we can go to get away from the Spirit of God. In the lowest of lows and the highest of heights, he is there. When your life circumstances feel heavy, dark, and hard, God is there. When you feel weary, exhausted, or broken, God is there.

God speaks in the darkness; it does not hinder him. He sustains you through it, comforts you, and mourns with you. His methods of relating may change, but his presence does not. Resist the temptation to equate hard times with the absence of God. A happy life in Christ is knowing that in darkness and in light, God is still speaking and moving.

What you hear from God, you are supposed to share. Dark seasons are not wasted. Jesus is speaking to you, advocating for you, and building you up. When you come out of the darkness, he wants you to tell others who may be in the dark the things he spoke to you. Isn't it beautiful that with God, no season is wasted? Tune your ear to hear in the darkness, and when you emerge, start to make known what was entrusted to you.

God thank you that you are ever near. You speak in the dark times and in the light, and you waste nothing in my life. Help me to proclaim your truth and goodness to those around me.

what I tell you in the dark, say in the light.

Matthew 10:27 ESV

Help at Hand

Every time they cried out to you in their despair,
you were faithful to deliver them;
you didn't disappoint them.

PSALM 22:5 TPT

Need a hand? When working on a project, who doesn't like to hear those words? It is a relief when someone offers to share your burden or workload. Jesus doesn't just want to share your burden; he wants to exchange his with you. And do you know how his is described? As easy. Light. Doesn't that sound like relief?

Whatever you are trying to do on your own today, stop and ask God to help you. He is willing and able to take your burden and bring relief and rest. Even the most faithful, loving friends and family will disappoint you at some time. It is inevitable. However, God is perfect, and he will never let you down. His Scripture is packed full of promises to never abandon you, always be faithful, and uphold and strengthen you. And that list is just a short one. It goes on and on.

God gives us relationships with others for many different reasons, but we can't put all our hope on those people. Our true hope can only rest in God. Make sure you have your relationships in their rightful place: God on the throne with all your trust in him, and people second.

Jesus, thank you that you are faithful; you never let me down. You offer to exchange your burden for mine. I want to lay this down. I need rest. Thank you for being faithful to deliver me. Thank you that you never disappoint me, and I can always rely on you.

Solid Ground

He lifted me out of the pit of despair,
out of the mud and the mire.
He set my feet on solid ground
and steadied me as I walked along.

PSALM 40:2 NLT

When you were a little kid, did you ever play sinking sand? It is a game that usually involves jumping from pillow to pillow or couch to couch because if you touch the ground, that's sinking sand! As adults we can fall into the routine of living the same way, jumping from one thing to the next, terrified of failure. Life in Christ doesn't need to be like this though.

No good pursuit or busy schedule is going to save you. A life built on the solid foundation of Jesus Christ is the only thing that will keep you grounded. He is the solid ground, steady and sure, and even if you fail, you can never mess up enough to sink.

Christ will lift you and set you on solid ground. He will steady you as you walk. Don't attempt to do it all in your strength. To get your act together and pull yourself out of the pit. Why strive when the all-powerful God is so near and willing to help? He wants to do things for you. Continue to walk, taking steps of faith, and submit your life to the power of the Holy Spirit.

Jesus, will you be my solid ground? I need stability and strength. I want to stop doing it on my own and rely on you. Thank you for your saving power.

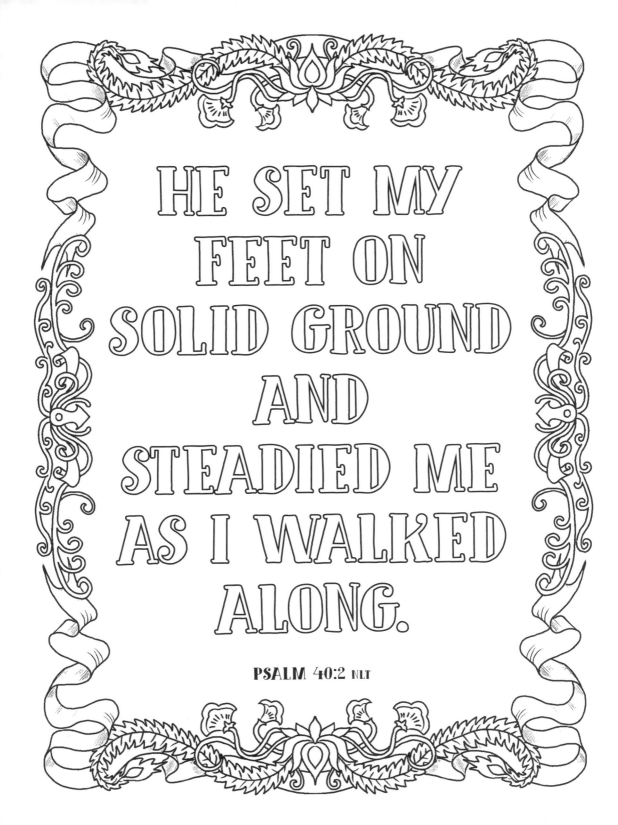

HE SET MY FEET ON SOLID GROUND AND STEADIED ME AS I WALKED ALONG.

PSALM 40:2 NLT

Shield around Me

You, O Lord, are a shield about me,
my glory, and the lifter of my head.

PSALM 3:3 ESV

Are you walking through life with your head down just trying to make it through? Some call that *survival mode*. God doesn't want you to just survive in this life; he wants you to thrive! Here God says that he is the lifter of your head. What a beautiful promise.

Lift your eyes for a moment and gaze into the eyes of your Father. Let his kindness break the chains that are weighing you down. Let him build up faith in you: a shield to protect you from the arrows of the enemy. Maybe you've had your shield down for too long now, and the bombardment of lies has caused your head to droop as well. Lift up your eyes! Lift up your shield! Let God restore your soul, so you thrive in the life he has called you to.

You may feel exhausted, but God does not grow weary. You may be at the end, but God is just getting started. You may feel exposed and in need of protection, but God's got you wrapped up safe. The battle belongs to God. Don't try to win it on your own. You can rest secure knowing that God is with you and he is protecting you. You are safe in his all-encompassing will.

God, will you lift my eyes? Will you show me that my help comes from you? Will you fight my battle? Can you comfort my soul? I need you now. Wrap me up safe and don't let me go.

YOU, O LORD, ARE A SHIELD ABOUT ME, MY GLORY, AND THE LIFTER OF MY HEAD.

PSALM 3:3 ESV

Light of Love

He has delivered us from the power of darkness
and conveyed us into the kingdom of the Son of His love.

COLOSSIANS 1:13 NKJV

God wants to bring all the dark places in you to light so he can heal them. Maybe you are holding tightly to something, trying to bury it deep. God desires for you to be wholly healthy. Your family needs you to be healthy. Your friends need you to pursue light. Your church body needs your testimony.

God is gracious and kind, and he will not force your hand. But if you choose to bring what you're most afraid of to the light, if you are willing to walk through the darkness, you will come out the other side in the most glorious brilliance. He will take the darkest parts of your story and give them light to give you healing and to give others hope. When they see and hear about the light in you, they will put their trust in the Lord. Stay tender to God's leading and hold his hand tight through the healing. Let your story be a light in someone else's darkness.

Have you ever heard of Seasonal Affective Disorder? Maybe you live in one of the more northern climates and are familiar with the term. It is a type of depression that is caused by winter seasons from the lack of sunlight. Some places don't see the sun for days on end. Biologically we are wired for light. Spiritually, we are too. We are made to be at home with Jesus in his kingdom of light. Living in his kingdom brings us to full health and wholeness.

God, thank you that you have brought me out of the dungeon and into glorious light! Heal my soul and make me whole in you.

Confident Hope

Faith is confidence in what we hope for
and assurance about what we do not see.

HEBREWS 11:1 NIV

The word *faith* can seem so abstract sometimes. It's a word you paint in calligraphy and hang on signs in your house, yet it feels a little ambiguous. So, what does it mean to have faith in God? To stand confidently in the knowledge that God exists, and he is at work.

If you struggle with the concept of faith as well, take heart that you can grow in it over time. It is a gift from God; step one is asking for it! Step two is acknowledging that you don't have to settle for the same amount of faith you've always had. Ask for more. Step three, let your faith be developed by trusting in God's ways. The ways you can see, and the ways that leave you with whys. All of these steps rely on God. Faith is for the wonderful seasons and downright challenging ones alike. Ask God today to fill you confidently with faith.

Confidence is trusting in Jesus. You have the assurance of who Jesus is and who you are to him. Your identity is completely wrapped up in him, and with Jesus as your source, you can walk out your days full of faith displayed for all to see. The power comes from the one who lives inside of you. Dare to live with faith and confidence today.

God, fill me with faith anew. Help me to trust in you. Keep building up faith in me. I love you!

Faith is confidence in what we hope for and assurance about what we do not see.

Hebrews 11:1 NIV

Fullness of Grace

Indeed, we have all received
grace upon grace from his fullness.

JOHN 1:16 CSB

God doesn't waste anything. Do you believe it? Life can leave us high and dry, too weary to face another day. The mundane circumstances you live in may seem useless. The trial you went through was too painful and overwhelming. The questions you are asking don't seem to be answered.

God is in the business of making all things new, and in this he doesn't waste one minute of your life. Imagine God as the painter, and you come to him hoping for a beautiful portrait but lacking in supplies. He has everything he needs; he is full of supplies to turn what you offer into the masterpiece canvas you hoped he would create.

Jesus is the man for the grace-giving job. Fully God and fully man, he was the only one with the means to conquer sin and death and create the pathway back to God. He's the only one who can give grace abundantly as you need it. How do you know that he is qualified? The Bible is the resume of his love, his character, and his working amongst humanity doing exactly this—handing out grace. Trust in this promise today.

Jesus, thank you for the grace you give. Thank you for being qualified and for giving your life for me. Thank you for not wasting anything. I need your grace now. Will you give me more?

Learning to Rest

For God alone, O my soul, wait in silence,
for my hope is from him.

PSALM 62:5 ESV

It seems like society is just speeding up. With the advance of technology, productivity soars, and a do-it-all attitude emerges. This is in direct contrast to the command in Scripture for rest. Even prayer and devotional time can become a to-do list, quickly reading, checking the box, and handing Jesus a checklist of requests. When was the last time you sat in silence in the presence of God?

Our instinct is to fill the void: grab our Bibles, pull out our phones, turn on music. We even have spiritual ways of avoiding silence. God is not afraid of the quiet. It takes courage to sit in the silence and wait on him. Rest is the resistance against a world that tells us we must do more to be worthy.

It doesn't need to be over-spiritualized. Although prayer and Bible reading are necessary and good, God invites us into rest in other ways as well. He is not limited to Sunday mornings and prayer closets. God has created so many things for us to enjoy, and each of us is unique. Some will find joy and refreshment in a long hike in the woods. Others will find it in a cozy coffee shop surrounded by people. God is not a merciless dictator. He wants you to delight in life. To see the beauty in the world around you. Rest will never run toward you and make you stop. You must pursue it.

God, thank you that you created a world for me to enjoy. Help me to learn the spiritual discipline of silence and rest.

MY HOPE IS FROM HIM.

PSALM 62:5 ESV

Seeing Goodness

I remain confident of this:
I will see the goodness of the LORD
in the land of the living.

PSALM 27:13 NIV

This verse is a foundational truth for anyone wanting a happy life. We must be firmly rooted in the fact that our God is good. Our view of God's goodness will completely shift our lives to either joy-filled living or despair. Our circumstances are always changing. There are inevitable things we cannot control. The surest footing we have is in Christ. Despair will swallow you whole if you put your trust in anything else.

Hope in God and know that he is in control. All his actions toward you are motivated by love, and he will give you joy in the here and now. The land of the living—that is this moment, this life. Do you believe God's goodness toward you? Are you sold on this truth?

There are a number of ways to help foster your belief in God's goodness. Have a love for his Word. Being familiar with the promises of God will empower you to see him acting, and it will build faith that he is true to who he says he is. Have a right view of his nature. Culture, upbringing, and experience can sometimes skew your perception of him. Make sure that how you view him is in line with how he truly is. Live with expectancy that he will move in your life. Make space for worship and prayer. Move forward in faith. You can experience the power of God and know his goodness.

God, thank you that you are good! Heal me of any skewed views of you. Let me see you rightly. Bring me joy in your presence here and now.

I remain confident of this: I will see the goodness of the LORD in the land of the living.

Psalm 27:13 NIV

Unload the Burdens

"Come to me, all you who are weary and burdened, and I will give you rest. Take my yoke upon you and learn from me, for I am gentle and humble in heart, and you will find rest for your souls."

Matthew 11:28-29 NIV

Are you so independent that you feel like you don't need anyone? Maybe you carry your independency as a badge of honor. Sometimes being independent can be positive but be quick to recognize any pride that may subtly be running in the background. You were not created to be an independent loner who has it all together. God created you to be in relationship. First with him, and second with others. That is how you thrive.

Trying to carry all life's troubles and the weight of sin yourself will lead to inevitable failure. You might be able to survive under the pressure for a while, but why? At what cost? In humility, come to Christ and lay it at his feet. Look at the body of Christ ready to help you, and trust God enough to be vulnerable with them. Rest and relationship wait for you.

The yoke in Matthew was a heavy, wooden device that hung on the necks of animals working in the fields. Trying to live perfectly is the yoke of the law, and living in sin is the yoke of bondage. A yoke is usually pulled by two animals. Instead of bearing the yoke alone, why not let Christ bear it with you or for you? Who better to be tethered to than him?

Jesus, thank you that you bear my burdens. Show me areas in my life where I am acting too independently. Walk with me today. I want to stay in step with you.

Even More

God gives us even more grace, as the Scripture says,
"God is against the proud, but he gives grace to the humble."

James 4:6 NCV

It seems like a no-brainer. Stubbornly continue in your own way, not asking for help and foolishly following your pride, and you won't receive grace. Or humble yourself, ask God for more, submit, and he will give it to you. Pride is the hardwiring of a fallen nature. It's the forefront of every sin. God has an abundance of grace available to you, but if you choose to do things your way, he's not going to force you to accept the grace.

Make it a daily practice to come before the Lord and humble yourself. It's as easy as a simple prayer. God will always answer your plea for grace. It is impossible that your need for grace is greater than God's supply. Walk in this world, but don't be of it (Romans 12:2). To do this, you need grace. It's the key.

Do you struggle with repeated sin, beating yourself up when you return to the same action or heart position once again? The question to ask yourself is how did you find forgiveness and grace for it the first time? You came to God and repented! Come again. And again. And for the rest of your life. Humble yourself before God and drink deep of the grace that he gives.

Jesus, make me humble before you. Help me not to walk in pride.

Positioned for Rescue

I am dying from grief;
my years are shortened by sadness.
Sin has drained my strength;
I am wasting away from within.

PSALM 31:10 NLT

The psalms can be likened to an emotional rollercoaster. That's reassuring for many who can relate. David was a king pursued by flesh-and-bone enemies, with assassination plots against his life, wars to fight, and a kingdom to run, but the emotions can be the same whether you're a barista, teacher, or flight attendant.

Sorrow and fear do not include or exclude based on wealth or position. When David had big feelings, he wasn't bemoaning them to his bestie. He didn't send out public decrees. He was at the feet of Jesus pouring out his soul. This is what put him in a position for rescue by the only one who could possibly save him. The same is available to you.

Do you air out your soul to others or to God?

When life's storms come, it's not helpful to continue on with business as usual, trying to convince yourself, God, and others that you are fine. When the storms come, position yourself for rescue. Move into a posture of prayer and worship. Cry out to your Savior. Bottling it all up and pressing on won't change anything. God is faithful to rescue you. Humbly submit yourself to his help.

God, I submit myself to you. Life is hard sometimes! The storm swirls around me. Will you rescue me? I know you will be faithful to do so.

Ask Again

Oh, that I might have my request,
and that God would fulfill my hope.

JOB 6:8 ESV

Did Job get it? You know, the one request that he wants to have fulfilled. Look around at the context: do we even get to know what this one request is? Perhaps the bigger question is does it really matter? What matters is the posture of Job's heart toward God.

In light of eternity, maybe it's not the subject of our prayers that holds the most significance, but it is the posture of our hearts. Do we turn to God in prayer, cry out to him, or have a heart of submission to his will? If the subject of our prayers becomes more important than who we are praying to, we've cheapened God to a glorified vending machine. First and foremost, God wants us to come to him in prayer with hearts that say, "Your will be done."

What is the one thing Job is asking for? It's that he might die before he ends up cursing God. Job isn't asking for relief from the trials, which is pretty surprising! When he prayed, he asked to bring glory to God through his suffering. He prayed that his heart would be soft toward God before he died. He had God in the right focus and his life in the right perspective. God doesn't promise us a suffering-free life, but he does promise to be with us through it all.

Jesus, I want you to be the main focus of my life. No matter what else is going on, may I bring glory to your name above all.

My Sustainer

Preserve me, O God,
For in You I put my trust.

PSALM 16:1 NKJV

When you are canning something, like fresh peaches, you have to listen for the pop. You have to get really still. You pull the jars out of the boiling water, set them on the counter and wait. You wait for the pop. If you hear it, you know that whatever is inside the jar will be preserved. Then it can sit on your shelf for quite some time, waiting to be enjoyed on a January day when you are cold and in need of some sunshine peaches. If the jar doesn't pop, the contents won't last long. It's not an extravagant sound like fireworks. It's subtle but sure.

In the same way, we need to get still before God and listen. What are we waiting for? The voice of God. This world is noisy and distracting. If we want to persevere until the end, we need to get still on a regular basis. Try and spend five minutes in the quiet, not asking God for anything, not singing or even reading, just being still, meditating on who God is, and listening for his voice.

Perseverance in the Christian faith is not just about gritting your teeth and pressing onward. To truly persevere, you need to fling yourself onto the only one who can sustain you. Maybe you feel like the weight of your life is too much to bear. Jesus can carry all that weight. He can sustain you through it all.

Jesus, you are my sustainer. I love you so much! You lift me up and carry me in my hardest situations. You are the one who makes me persevere.

He Can Take It

Give all your worries and cares to God,
for he cares about you.

1 PETER 5:7 NLT

If you've ever been around a toddler, you'll know that most go through a bag phase. It's a phase where one of their favorite toys is any bag or bucket you can find. They spend their time toddling around on their tiny legs, collecting random artifacts from around the house and placing them in their bag. Temper tantrums ensue if the bag can no longer be carried. What they don't realize is they probably collected more stuff than they themselves weigh! Over the course of their playtime, the load became too heavy.

We operate in a similar fashion. Perhaps we are familiar with this verse about handing our concerns to Christ; maybe we've even prayed and done so recently. Sometimes we go about our normal routines not even realizing that we are grabbing burdens and holding on to them, weighing ourselves down. Then, we get to a point where we are overwhelmed, and we wonder how our bag got so heavy. Casting your cares on Christ is a daily practice. It's an awareness of what you are taking on, and a constant submission to handing it over.

If anyone can handle your problem, don't you think it would be your all-powerful, all-knowing God? Acknowledge that his ways are higher and better than yours. Be careful not to micromanage him. He knows the big picture, the whole story. He's got this. You can let go.

Jesus, help me to let go of the things I'm clinging to and give them to you. Help me not to pick them back up again but to trust in you for my future.

Give all
your worries
and cares to God,
for he cares
about you.

1 Peter 5:7 NLT

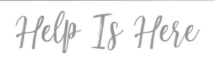

Help Is Here

From the depths of despair, O Lᴏʀᴅ,
I call for your help.
Pꜱᴀʟᴍ 130:1 ɴʟᴛ

There is no such thing as rock bottom when it comes to Christ. You can feel like you are there, for sure, but it will never be far enough that God cannot reach you. When you mess up, you might shy away from God in shame. You run the opposite direction and assume that you've done too much—that God can't love you anymore. That couldn't be further from the truth.

Jesus, when he died, descended all the way into hell. That's about as far as you can go! But he didn't stay there. No, he conquered hell, death, and sin, and reclaimed you as his own. There is no depth too deep that Christ cannot find you and pull you out. Next time you are tempted to turn away from God, turn in to him instead. He's there, waiting, and there is no place he won't go to redeem you.

If you aren't experiencing difficulty today, pray and ask God who you can reach out to. There are so many different ways people can be in deep despair. Often it's hard to see from the surface level. Find a way to encourage whoever the Lord puts on your heart. A handwritten note, a meal, a visit, the smallest actions can go a long way. While you are connecting, ask if you can pray for God to be near to them.

God, thank you that you are near. You help us when we cry out to you. Please lead me to those who need your help.

From the depths
of despair, O Lord,
I call for your help.

Psalm 130:1 NLT

No Need to Despair

Don't worry, because I am with you.
Don't be afraid, because I am your God.
I will make you strong and will help you;
I will support you with my right hand that saves you.

ISAIAH 41:10 NCV

The subject of these verses is not us, it's God. When he is our source, we cannot fail. We must shift our focus off ourselves and on to him. We could easily read this verse and make it all about us: how God will make us strong, help us, and lead us away from fear or worry. All of this is true and wonderful. But the real subject of these verses is God. He is doing all the heavy lifting.

God is our everything. He takes on so many roles in our lives and gives us many great things; we cannot help but be in awe of him. Turn your gaze to God. Spend time praising and thanking him.

It's good to realize your limits and appreciate that God has none. He can be the one supporting, guiding, crushing fear, and dissolving worry all in the same moment because he is limitless. As a finite human, it would serve you well to take on a more child-like posture of dependency on him instead of attempting to do everything yourself.

God, I praise you for how powerful and awesome you are. I am in awe of all you do. I confess I try to do too much too often. Will you forgive me? I want to be dependent on you.

Radiant Hope

The Lord alone is our radiant hope
and we trust in him with all our hearts.
His wrap-around presence will strengthen us.

Psalm 33:22 tpt

During the coldest time of the year, you probably want to do nothing but sit in front of a roaring fire, with a steaming mug of coffee in hand, wrapped in the coziest of blankets. Doesn't that sound lovely? That cozy, restful picture of warmth is what comes to mind at the last section of this psalm.

The wrap-around presence speaks of the complete warmth and peace that comes from Christ. His love toward you surrounds you in the best possible way. And it's not through working harder that you get strength; it's being enveloped in Christ's love and rest that does.

In seasons of winter, your view may be bleak, the air full of a hostile chill, and darkness comes quickly. Maybe your outlook on the state of the world could be described as dim hope. Shift your view to Christ, your radiant hope. Radiant light is warm, stunning, and all encompassing. It fills, leaving no area untouched. The light of Christ cannot be extinguished. He is in control, and he makes all things new. Praise him for this hope!

Jesus, thank you for your light that brings hope when the world seems dark. Thank you for rest that strengthens and surrounds me. You provide for all my needs.

Love Pours In

Hope does not put us to shame, because God's love has been poured into our hearts through the Holy Spirit who has been given to us.

ROMANS 5:5 ESV

Most people like to win (there's nothing wrong with that!), and hope can sometimes feel like a game. It's a gamble really, to hope, and no one wants to come out on the other side as a loser after throwing all their eggs into one basket. Shame is the flavor of the taste of defeat, and nobody is asking to lick that bowl after it's whipped up.

As children of God we have a hope that is sweeter than any other. After God's love has been poured in, after the seal of the Holy Spirit, there is no chance of you ending up on the losing side. The hope of Jesus cannot be defeated, and it makes your life a sweet aroma. Rejoice that your hope is everlasting and steadfast.

Now that you have the confidence of being on the winning side of eternity, what are you going to do with this knowledge? God's love has been poured into you to fill you and for you to pour out. You are a vessel of this hope to those around you. Don't be fooled by people who seem to have it all together. They think they have no need for Christ, but they really have no idea. If their hope is not in him, then whatever it is in will fail them eventually. As a believer, you have true hope. Share it loudly and proudly with your circle of influence today!

Jesus, thank you for giving me hope that does not disappoint. Help me to share this exciting, wonderful news with everyone around me, no matter how I view them in the moment.

Limitless

Your mercy, LORD, extends to the heavens,
Your faithfulness reaches to the skies.

PSALM 36:5 NASB

Have you ever felt pushed to the end of your rope? You realize you don't have capacity to extend grace or kindness. Often it is a passing feeling, one that simply takes getting recharged to fix. God is limitless. He never runs out of love for you. He never thinks that you are too much. He is never at a loss for what to do. He never decides to leave you. He never needs a time of separation from you. His kindness is so extensive, there is nothing you can do to make it end.

The tenderness and consideration of the Lord toward you extends far beyond what your human eye can see. It stretches to the heavens. The loyalty of God starts at you and is as tall as the clouds. If you could really get it nestled into your soul that God is limitlessly tender and compassionate toward you, what would it change in your life?

Sometimes life circumstances speak otherwise. Maybe you've hoped for something for so long and haven't achieved it. Or you've lost someone you love, or you've entered into a circumstance that has you asking why. It can be easy to let the tiny seed be planted in your heart that God is cruel and uncaring. Be on guard against this. The truth is that he is a tender, loving, considerate God.

God, help me to see you as you really are. Help me to know your true character and to trust you. Thank you for your lovingkindness.

New Life Coming

To all who mourn in Israel,
he will give a crown of beauty for ashes,
a joyous blessing instead of mourning,
festive praise instead of despair.
In their righteousness, they will be like great oaks
that the LORD has planted for his own glory.

ISAIAH 61:3 NLT

This is the great exchange. Close your eyes and picture it. Picture yourself surrounded by ashes. Imagine all the dirt and sorrow that such a picture entails. Then imagine Jesus cleansing you, giving you a crown; your surroundings are changed to a beautiful flower garden instead of an ash heap.

Let it be known, God is in the business of restoration. It's one of the very things he does best. God is not satisfied with leaving you in your current state. You could also say he is not satisfied with just removing your sin, though that is an awesome victory he has won for you! He wants to make all things new. He wants to restore and redeem.

What area of your life needs this promise today? There is no area too difficult, no sin too deep, no life too far gone for God to restore it. Won't you ask him to move in your life today?

God, will you restore to me what has been stolen? I long to see your restoration power in my life.

Everything I Need

"The LORD is my portion," says my soul,
"therefore I will hope in him."

LAMENTATIONS 3:24 ESV

When having guests over, or perhaps even just feeding your own family, it's wise to consider portions. Some come to the table hungry every time, and you learn that you need to have more food available for them. Others come and peck around, maybe dissatisfied with what's being served or just not as eager to eat. When someone comes who is hungry, it's pretty inevitable that they will get more food. As they should!

The Lord is your portion. Are you coming to the table hungry, or distracted and peckish? If you're hungry for the things of the Lord, he is faithful to give you more. Consider your stance today. If you're hungry, tell God. Ask for more. It delights him to give to those who are hungry. If your posture is different, try searching your heart to see what ways you could be filling your appetite with things that won't sustain your soul.

A life of thankfulness leads to contentment, and a life of contentment is a life of happiness. You can find everything you need in Christ. Learning to be thankful for the everyday gifts of God will fill you with contentment.

Jesus, thank you for all your gifts. Create in me a renewed hunger for the things that build your kingdom. My hope is in you.

Hope Is Here

I rise before the dawning of the morning,
And cry for help;
I hope in Your word.

PSALM 119:147 NKJV

Here you are. Sure, it might not be before dawn, but you're sitting here expectant. Maybe it's still dark outside, or it's late enough that you could have brunch. No matter the situation, soaking in God's Word shows you are someone who puts their hope in the Word of God. In order to live, you need his Word. It's better than a fresh cup of coffee, more sustaining than a hearty breakfast. It's encouraging just to be in God's Word for a moment. Everything you need for life and godliness is available to you there. Open it up, soak it in, and ask His Spirit to guide you.

No matter what stage or circumstance you find yourself in, hope is present. It's as simple as crying out in prayer. As simple as opening God's Word and meditating on it. The more you ingest it, the healthier you get. You can never have too much. The more you read it, the more it gets committed to memory.

When you have God's Word memorized, you can access hope no matter where you are. It helps you dispose of the lies you once believed. It squelches the fears you let grow for too long, and it uproots bitterness that has gotten so deep. It calms anxieties that threaten to overrun you and provides wisdom when you feel fresh out. And that's only the beginning. Seek health in your spiritual life by actively seeking God's Word.

Jesus, let your Word take root in my heart. Expel the lies that I've taken in and let truth flourish!

I rise before the dawning of the morning, And cry for help; I hope in Your word.

Psalm 119:147 NKJV

Love Covers Everything

He escorts me to the banquet hall;
it's obvious how much he loves me.

Song of Solomon 2:4 NLT

We use banners at parties to declare things. Sometimes they are as simple as a banner that states "Happy Birthday!" Other times, more intimate and personalized messages can be conveyed. Banners are usually large—visible when you walk into a room. If the banner says, "Happy birthday, Jane!" you know how to interact with Jane: you wish her a happy birthday!

God's banner over you is love. Written over you is his endless love. It is your status and your truth. You are loved by God. This is far better than any earthly love. It knows you to the depths of your soul, inside and out, and still loves. Because love is God's banner over you, you can let it shine through you to others.

Imagine yourself with a large banner written over you that says, "Loved by God!" You're in a big celebration hall. But you showed up in rags. Sitting under that banner, wouldn't you feel a little self-conscious? We often approach our relationship with God this way. He says that we are loved, pure, and cleansed by the blood of his Son, yet we still think we are sitting in rags, completely out of place. Self-conscious in our state, we fail to believe that what the banner says is true. We must reshape our thoughts to see ourselves how God sees us. We must cling tightly to the truth of Scripture.

God, it amazes me that you would put a banner of love over me. You love me deeply. Thank you for this truth! Help me to see myself how you see me.

He Sees Me

The needy will not be ignored forever;
the hopes of the poor will not always be crushed.

PSALM 9:18 NLT

We've all been there. It's not a good feeling to be overlooked or underappreciated. The loneliness that settles in can feel like it has suppressed all hope or joy. Though we cannot expect to never experience this from other humans, we can expect to never experience it from God. God turned away from Jesus on the cross so that he never has to turn away from you.

Even in your lowest of states, your messiest of problems, or just your mundane life, he sees you. He notices your struggle. He sees your pain. He delights in your rejoicing. Having the Holy Spirit living in you means you have God as your constant companion. If you woke up today feeling crushed, take heart. God sees you with eyes full of love and compassion, and he is leaning toward you, wanting to hear what you have to say.

To be seen is to be known. Do you feel known by God? What is holding you back? Though God is all-knowing, he is also a gentleman. He will not force his way into places you refuse to open up to him. Jesus is standing at the door, knocking, but your belief is what opens the door. The encouragement is that he's not here to criticize; he's here to renew. What a beautiful hope that is!

Holy Spirit, I submit my life to you. Come in and remodel! Make me more like you. Heal the broken parts of me; restore to me the things that sin has stolen. Thank you for your kindness and for the hope that I can be in relationship with you.

Never-ending Help

Do not worry about anything,
but pray and ask God for everything you need,
always giving thanks.

PHILIPPIANS 4:6 NCV

Humans seem to have a default mode of worrying or fixing. When we need something, we either spend our time worrying about it or trying to fix it. Philippians tells us God's way to do things. Pray. It takes spiritual discipline to make prayer your default, but it is something you can grow in.

God is able to meet every need you have. Physical, spiritual, emotional, financial—he's got it. The lack is not on his end, it's on ours for not asking. Imagine you had a child, and the child was hungry. You're sitting at the table with the food already made, but the child keeps trying to make his own food out of wood blocks. That's crazy, right? That's how we often act around God. What do you need today? Confidently ask him.

The third section of this verse is just as important as the first two—give thanks. Always. Constantly. Does it feel a little overwhelming when you see the word *always*? Paul is simply stating that we can choose to have a lifestyle that breathes thanks to God. If you want happiness in Jesus, gratitude is the sure-fire way to get there. It is a form of worship that will unlock countless benefits in your life. Every time you find yourself latching onto something to worry about, flip it around, find gratitude in it, and pray about it. Watch your life change!

Jesus, thank you for providing for all my needs. Help me grow in the discipline of having gratitude.

Do not worry about anything, but pray and ask God for everything you need, always giving thanks.

Philippians 4:6 NCV

Everlasting Life

These things I have written to you who believe in the name of the Son of God, that you may know that you have eternal life, and that you may continue to believe in the name of the Son of God.

1 John 5:13 NKJV

Some of us have been raised believing that faith in Jesus is a one-time deal. You hear the gospel, say the sinner's prayer, and that's it! You've gained your ticket to heaven, and you can go on living however you please. That is just a partial truth. Upon hearing the gospel and feeling the conviction of the Holy Spirit for sin, it is as simple as praying to Jesus to save you. But then, God is not done giving you grace with that one-time transaction. You must continue to believe. It doesn't mean that you can slip up and lose your salvation if you have a rough day, but God wants you to continue to apply his grace to your life daily. Coming to faith in Jesus should change your life and continue to change it until you die.

When you first believe in Jesus, there is an excitement and a newness about it that inspires you. But as the years go by, doubts can grow, and continuing to live in a godless world can take its toll. You may start to wonder about the faith you found.

It's important to be in God's Word, praying to find encouragement and perseverance. It's also important to have spiritual mentors in the faith who can help you when times get tough. If you don't have anyone, pray about who you could ask to partner with you in faith, and continue to believe in the name of Jesus.

Jesus, thank you for the assurance of salvation. Help me to grow in faith and to continue to believe.

Met By Mercy

Let us come boldly to the throne of our gracious God.
There we will receive his mercy,
and we will find grace to help us when we need it most.

HEBREWS 4:16 NLT

When someone has a history of being short with people—angry, frustrated, or mean—we would tend to avoid approaching that person. We would walk on eggshells or make sure we came at what seemed to be the most ideal time. We tiptoe around in relationships with people who lie a lot or who are manipulative. There is no trust in the relationship. Can it even be called a relationship?

Think about your relationship with God. Do you view him as angry? Do you think you always need to approach him with hesitation? Maybe you're unsure if he has your best interest in mind. What lie about the character of God is holding you back from entering into his presence? If something is making you hesitant to come to him, you can be sure it is a lie. Search your heart today, ask God to reveal to you what lies about his character you may be believing.

Scripture is full of tools to help you rightly align your thinking. What joy awaits you in the presence of God! Abundant mercy, rivers of grace, buckets of joy, an atmosphere of love—where else would you want to be? Do you need mercy, love, grace, or strength? It's there. Everything you could possibly need is available from your loving Father. Approach, ask, and receive.

Father, thank you that we can come boldly to your throne. Help me identify any lies that are holding me back from you. Thank you for providing everything I could ask for or need.

Rewards

Don't lose your bold, courageous faith,
for you are destined for a great reward!

HEBREWS 10:35 TPT

The parable of the pearl of great price and the treasure hidden in a field are stories Jesus told to illustrate the importance of what he was buying for us on the cross. Our very great reward is eternal life: a life free of sin, forever united with Christ.

Jesus says we can gain the whole world and lose our soul, or it can be the opposite. This reward is worth losing our very lives over. It is the most prized treasure. If all this is true, what would you give it away for? A few nights of pleasure? A comfortable and secure physical life? Count the cost and choose to follow Christ. You will never regret it.

Jesus is worth it. He is higher than anything you can lose. Maybe you are having a hard time reckoning with that truth. Take some time to contemplate the price that Jesus paid to bring you into his kingdom, the glorious nature of what he promises you when you follow him, and the wonder of Jesus himself. He is your very great reward. Let God minister the reassurance of who he is to your heart.

Jesus, thank you. You are my great reward. You died on the cross and paid the highest price for me. Where I'm having a hard time letting go, show me your patience, your goodness, and your glory.

Calmed by Comfort

When anxiety was great within me,
your consolation brought me joy.

PSALM 94:19 NIV

On a computer internet browser, you can have many tabs open at the same time. Each tab can hold a different website. Browser brain is when your brain feels like it is doing that exact same thing—tabs of cares, worries, anxieties all running and taking up space at once. Some people have also called it popcorn brain: where worries are popping up in your brain constantly. Whichever visual picture you choose, the point is that it can be overwhelming!

In these times we can choose two paths of comfort. The first is to remember past experience. If you've been a believer for any length of time, you have already encountered God's faithfulness. Look back and remember. He has never failed you or abandoned you, and he won't start now. Secondly, remember his promises toward you in his Word. He has promised to heal you, to be near to you, to redeem and restore you. These two forms of comfort can be the consolation that closes all the browsers and stops the popcorn, leaving you with peace of mind.

It is one thing to be at rest, it is another level to have joy. Biblically speaking, joy can be described as the confidence that God is in control of your life, so you know everything will be ok. It takes determination to find a heart of praise after you've been attacked by anxiety. But when gratitude and admiration for God take the forefront of your thoughts, then anxiety has no choice but to be silent.

God, thank you that you are in control. Help me to quiet my thoughts; remove anxiety from me.

Not Done Yet

Rejoice in hope, be patient in tribulation, be constant in prayer.

ROMANS 12:12 ESV

A prayerless life is spiritual suicide. So, why do surveys show that it is one of the most neglected spiritual disciplines amongst believers? We are exhorted several times in Scripture to remain in prayer. Here in Romans it says our prayers should be constant. In the Old Testament, God was only accessible through priests and sacrifices or on less frequent occasions, when an angel or God himself appeared or spoke. Since Christ's resurrection, we have been given the gift of the Holy Spirit and have full access to the throne of God.

What is holding you back? Do you feel discouraged because you've prayed in the past and haven't seen anything happen? Do you struggle to believe God is near? The words of Paul seem simple enough when etched at the top of this page yet putting them into practice is something else entirely! It's important to see that our rejoicing, patience, and consistent prayer all point to the fact that God is not done yet. He is still working and moving in our world.

Our hope is in the fact that this world is not our home. Our earthly life is the journey, not the destination. Constant prayer keeps us connected and in relationship with our God who is at work. He will keep us in tune with what his plan is and what he is doing when we spend time seeking him.

God, you aren't done yet, and I praise you for that! Help me to be patient in hard times. To find joy in my eternal hope. Thank you for listening to me.

We're Already In

Fear of the Lord leads to life
bringing security and protection from harm.

PROVERBS 19:23 NLT

As advertisements go, Proverbs 19:23 puts forth a rather persuasive pitch for joining your life to God's. Abundant life? Yes, please! Continual protection? Let us in! Complete satisfaction? Where do we sign? Here's the best part of all: we already signed. We're already in. The day we fell in love with Jesus and asked him into our hearts, all this and more was ours. To claim it, we need only remain in his love. To experience it, we need only give the Father our awe.

When we are reclined on the beach, hearing gentle waves rhythmically hit the shore, the ocean doesn't seem particularly fearsome. Jumping from a ship into twelve-foot swells and with no land in sight? It's hard to imagine anything more terrifying. It's a matter of perspective. From land, it's easy to forget the ocean's vastness and power. From the center, it's impossible to think of anything else.

This is what it means to fear God. To fear him is to respect him—to remember his vastness, to stand in awe of his power. Let us remain at the center of our faith, constantly aware of all he can, has, and will do, and find our secure rest there.

God, thank you for letting me in on the best deal ever. An overflowing life, completely safe and satisfying, is more than I could hope for before I met you; now it's mine to live and to share. What an awesome, generous God you are!

Fear of the
Lord leads
to life,
bringing
security and
protection
from harm.

Proverbs 19:23 NLT

Heart Directions

*May the Lord direct your hearts to the love of God
and to the steadfastness of Christ.*

2 Thessalonians 3:5 esv

Popular culture says the key to happiness is to follow your heart. The idea is that by pursuing our passions, we're most likely to end up in a good place. It seems like lovely advice, but only as long as we're sure our hearts know the way. Could your heart use directions from time to time?

A young woman choosing partying with friends over hard work or study, or a middle-aged, married woman acting on a flirtation that makes her heart flutter—both women could be following their hearts. Yet the heart can be deceptive. The heart's wants can be based on selfish, unhealthy, or irresponsible desires. God's heart, though, is steady and true. He knows exactly where we need to go.

Visit any public venue and you're likely to see a child sprinting away from their parents. Their excitement can't be contained in their little bodies. They bolt because they are so certain they know where to go. We hear their harried parents call out. "Slow down!" Whether by allowing her to temporarily believe she is lost, or by explaining the potential dangers of running off, the parents will try and teach her to stay close. We know the Lord has plans for us, so each time we think we see a glimpse of what's next, we bolt. No looking left and right, no checking the rearview mirror, we just go. "Slow down," our Savior calls. May we listen and learn to stay close.

God, direct my heart. Lead me toward purpose and stability.

Pain Has Purpose

Jesus answered, "It was neither that this man sinned, nor his parents; but it was so that the works of God might be displayed in him."

JOHN 9:3 NASB

In Jesus' time, it was common to believe people with afflictions were being punished for either their own sins or those of a family member. Among the many incredible lessons about the heart of God that Jesus taught, he also set the record straight on this account. The man, blind since birth, was sightless so that everyone witnessing—and everyone who would ever read this story—would see the awesome power of God. Pain has purpose. It draws us to the Father and gives us a chance to experience his compassion and healing. It may feel like punishment but believe Jesus' words: it's not.

Stories like the one in the verse above may seem unfair. If we have been in our own season of affliction, we may even think God is being cruel. This poor man had to spend his entire life blind just so Jesus could perform a miracle? Ask yourself, though, what the man would say.

Always in darkness, he met Jesus who brought him into the light. The first face he ever saw was that of the Son of God. The hands who healed him were the hands of the Christ. Do you suppose he'd tell you it was worth it?

Father, I know you don't punish me. Things beyond my control and messes I get into all on my own are opportunities for me to witness all you are able to do. Don't let me be blinded by pain. Show me your glory and restore my sight.

Light in Darkness

*In him was life, and that life was the light of all mankind.
The light shines in the darkness,
and the darkness has not overcome it.*

JOHN 1:4-5 NIV

Unless you are trying to sleep, what is the first thing you look for in the dark? Light. We require illumination to find our way. When light and dark are used figuratively, the same truth applies. There is a reason a tough season is referred to as a dark time. It's hard to see the way through. Obstacles are everywhere.

In our own darkness, Jesus is a constant source of life-giving, soul-nurturing light. He is likewise constant for all those who love him. For those who have yet to know him, let us be light. Let us bring his words, his presence, and his peace everywhere we go.

In God's creation, total darkness is rare. Halfway around the world, the sun still finds a way—on all but the cloudiest of nights—to reflect off the moon. The lights of a billion stars, unfathomably far away, still make their way to earth. There is always a little light because light is stronger than the dark. In the darkest room, a single candle will change everything. It doesn't matter how dark that room is meant to be, that tiny flame will always succeed. As long as it's there, the room cannot be shrouded in darkness.

Because you never leave me, God, I am never lost in darkness. I need only turn to face you. As you are ever with me, I can also light someone's way. Thank you for your constant glow.

Loving Intercession

We constantly pray for you, that our God may make you worthy of his calling, and that by his power he may bring to fruition your every desire for goodness and your every deed prompted by faith.

2 Thessalonians 1:11 NIV

Do you have someone who often tells you they are praying for you? Maybe a parent, a sibling, or a close friend? What a gift they are! Since they have a heart to see you thrive, why not help them by sharing your God-given dreams with them?

We know the Lord answers the prayers of the faithful, so as we invite others to pray for us, we can be confident he will hear them. Our desire to find and fulfill our purpose, our longing to be worthy of the great love of Christ, and the acts we perform in obedience to his calling: all will be blessed by their loving intercession. We are wired for connection. We are called to intercede for one another. We are made for love. Do you believe this?

To study God's Word with others and encourage each other to grow in faith is a beautiful, life-giving experience. Having people who constantly pray for you—and having people to constantly pray for—is a wonderful gift. As we take our eyes our own concerns to lift up those of our friends, the Lord sees and rewards our compassion. As we share the load together, our burdens grow lighter.

God, thank you for those who pray for me. I don't want to take them for granted. Knowing they want to see me reach my every dream is a gift. Having their sincere prayers for my growth and success is a blessing. Hear their prayers.

Wide Open

Though you have not seen Him, you love Him, and though you do not see Him now, but believe in Him, you greatly rejoice with joy inexpressible and full of glory.

1 Peter 1:8 NASB

What are your thoughts on love at first sight? Does a soul recognize its other half instantly, or are we stitched together with our mates slowly over time? How about love in the absence of sight? Could you fall for someone based solely on the words he wrote to you and the things he did for you, even if you never saw his face?

Of course, you can, and you have. The day you fell in love with Jesus, the eyes of your heart were flung wide open. Though you won't lay eyes on him until you meet in heaven, your soul has already seen his beauty and found its missing half.

This beautiful picture of love is also a picture of faith. It is through faith we can rejoice in a promise. Trust allows us to revel in that we have yet to witness. We believe he is who he says he is, and believing, we love. Oh, how we love. And how he loves us for it! We didn't ask for proof, we just opened our hearts and let truth in. We didn't demand evidence; our souls simply accepted what he offered, and we loved. How can this be? How can we, doubting and fickle, have such great capacity for love and faith? Only through him. In this truth, we find yet another reason to love.

Oh, Jesus, how I love you! The most beautiful thing I'll ever see is something I've never seen at all, and yet I know it will be amazing. My heart knows. Oh, what inexpressible joy I will feel the day I see you face-to-face.

Unshakeable

I know how to live on almost nothing or with everything. I have learned the secret of living in every situation, whether it is with a full stomach or empty, with plenty or little. For I can do everything through Christ, who gives me strength.

PHILIPPIANS 4:12-13 NLT

Can you imagine feeling at peace no matter what circumstances you're in? Whether laid off, promoted, proposed to, dumped, selected, or rejected, you remain faithful and content? That kind of unshakeable peace seems extraordinary, perhaps even impossible, yet it's ours to take hold of.

Paul, after learning about this incredible gift, decided it was too wonderful to remain hidden. In the middle of his letter to the Philippians, he passed it along to them. Jesus is our supply. Whether we need help staying hopeful, or staying humble, the Lord gives us the strength.

Want to be unshakeable? Get your strength from Christ. When your source of power comes from him instead of your wallet, abilities, or the mirror, the supply is constant. There are no blackouts and no surges, just a steady stream.

With your faith resting securely in him, discontentment cannot gain a foothold. When your identity comes from his greatness, ego can't take any ground. The Lord is constant, and so is his peace. He is consistent, and so is his supply.

God, I confess I find this easier to believe on the good days than the tough ones. Whether from a prison cell, a hospital bed, or feeling alone and forgotten, let me boast of your sustaining peace.

Power and Grace

He said to me, "My grace is sufficient for you, for my power is made perfect in weakness." Therefore I will boast all the more gladly about my weaknesses, so that Christ's power may rest on me.

2 Corinthians 12:9 niv

Picture a tug-of-war contest. One side, all burly athletes, is dominating the other, a group of children. Which side would you be most inclined to jump in and help? Who would be more appreciative? God loves to come alongside us in all our endeavors, but he especially enjoys helping us when we are overpowered.

When we are feeling perfectly capable on our own, we are far less likely to appreciate—or even notice—the Lord's assistance. When we are outmanned, unqualified, and unprepared, his help is obvious and welcome. Be on the lookout for moments that were "all him," and give him the glory he deserves.

Hidden in the final words of this verse is a remarkable concept. Why would we boast about our weaknesses? So that the power of Christ may dwell in us. If admitting we sometimes struggle to be patient, occasionally fail to hold our tongue, and often feel incapable of loving the way we should will invite Jesus to send his power, let the confessions begin. As he helps us conquer these challenges, let our lives be a billboard for his power and grace.

Father, thank you for all the ways you help me. I'm sure I'm not aware of all you do but I certainly notice when you intervene and make me kinder, stronger, more patient, or more capable than usual. Your grace is sufficient, and I am more than grateful.

My grace is sufficient for you.

2 Corinthians 12:9 NIV

Many Parts

If the whole body were an eye, it would not be able to hear. If the whole body were an ear, it would not be able to smell. If each part of the body were the same part, there would be no body. But truly God put all the parts, each one of them, in the body as he wanted them.

1 CORINTHIANS 12:17-18 NCV

It's nearly impossible to experience a spectacular display of talent—whether painting, song, novel, or even a touchdown run—and not feel a longing to be able to perform at that same level. A captivating speaker is bound to make us yearn for the podium. A beautiful dance may stir us to dig out the old pink slippers. These feelings are both natural and a lovely tribute to the way God gifted the artists.

The important thing is not to become fixated on someone else's gifts, lest we miss out on discovering our own. If a mediocre singer at best is obsessed with becoming a vocalist, she may never realize her potential as a chef, nurse, or accountant. The world needs you to use the gifts you do have far more than to work on acquiring the ones you wish you had.

Imagine a country with nothing but athletes, a state with only doctors, or a city with only singers. It's unthinkable, almost laughable. No great athlete can become so without coaches, teachers, groundskeepers, equipment designers, assembly line workers, farmers, and so on. We need each other. Even right now, someone else's greatness depends on yours.

Father God, thank you for the way you made me. By making everyone unique, you ensure a world of endless delights, provision, and beauty.

How Eager

"What no eye has seen, nor ear heard, nor the heart of man imagined, what God has prepared for those who love him."

1 CORINTHIANS 2:9 ESV

Recall the most stunning sunset you've seen. Mentally replay the most gorgeous piece of music you've heard. Sit with these sensations for a moment. Now consider this: what you saw and what you heard are paltry compared to what the Lord has waiting for you in heaven. He can't wait to reveal it to you.

Every sense will be completely dazzled by the glory of heaven. Our minds can't comprehend it; we can't even dream it. The most delicious feasts, the most luxurious textures, and the most divine fragrances we've experienced so far will seem bland, scratchy, and faint next to the glories of God's kingdom.

When expecting a special guest, we take extra care in our preparations, fresh sheets, soft towels, and a fridge filled with favorites. We plan meaningful activities, fluff the pillows, and light a fire. God is infinitely more excited and immeasurably more prepared for our homecoming than we could be for any guest. He knows exactly what moves us, what stirs us, what overwhelms our hearts with joy, and having collected all those things together, he's going to multiply them and then multiply them again. That's how much God longs for us to come home.

God, the beauty I've experienced here on earth is so sublime that I can't imagine how much better things could be. What sounds more beautiful than a symphony? What scent is sweeter than a field of flowers? Yet you promise the best is yet to come. I can't wait to see what you've prepared.

Founded on Faith

"The rain came down, the streams rose,
and the winds blew and beat against that house; yet it did not fall,
because it had its foundation on the rock."

Matthew 7:25 NIV

Life's most difficult situations are often compared to storms. Considering the passage above, it's easy to see why. Issues pour upon us, calamities rise around us, and problems beat against us—sometimes all at once. These tough times are when our faith is tested, when we learn how solid our foundation is. If we rely on our own strength or count on others to be our source of stability, we may be flattened once the clouds recede.

A life founded on faith in God, built according to his Word and assembled with his truth, is solid and able to withstand even the strongest of storms. We may be battered, but we will still be standing. With Christ as our foundation, strong and certain, we remain upright.

How did you respond the last time you went through a storm? Were you fearful, or faithful; panicked, or patient; desperate, or devout? Don't think of this as a time to be self-critical, but instead as an invitation to become more self-aware. If illness sends you into a spiral of fear, or bad news produces a storm of short-temperedness, this may be the Lord's way of telling you it's time to restructure. The more your life is built on believing God, learning his Word, and following his ways, the steadier you will remain in a trial.

Lord Jesus, I will build my life on you. Your Word will be my cornerstone, and your sacrifice and grace my pillars. Whatever the storm, whatever the test, I'll remain because you remain.

Get Wisdom

"The beginning of wisdom is: acquire wisdom;
and with all your acquiring, get understanding."

PROVERBS 4:7 NCV

Can you imagine needing to understand or explain traffic if all the lights were shades of green? If it's grass-green, go ahead. If it's lime-green, you'd better hurry because once it gets to pine-green, you have to stop. We'd all be hopelessly confused.

Green means go. Red means stop. This basic pattern is one that is easily taught and learned even for young children. Our safety depends on understanding and following this system, so it was designed to be simple. While a lot of the Bible is poetic and symbolic, certain instructions, like this one, are as straightforward as a stoplight. Why? Because they're that important. Wisdom? It's a really big deal.

Solomon, widely attributed to be the wisest man who ever lived, goes out of his way to emphasize the value of wisdom. Nothing matters more. Start here. His urging reflects the importance of constantly seeking greater understanding. If we want to have something, we need to go get it. Want to be strong? Start exercising frequently. Want to be fast? Go for a run every day. Want to be wise? Learn from every experience.

God, thank you for making sure I can't miss the big lessons. Because you want me safe and wise, you make your most important instructions the easiest to follow. Help me get wisdom. Thank you for reminding me how much it matters.

Source of Peace

Those who love your instructions have great peace
and do not stumble.

PSALM 119:165 NLT

If you could be guaranteed a lifetime of peace with only one small requirement, would you be interested? According to this Scripture, you can. If you love the Lord's law, you will have great peace. Can this be possible? Rule-following sounds anything but peaceful; it sounds tedious and difficult. Following rules can be exhausting but, mercifully, that is not what it means to love the law.

Loving God's law means trusting his will for your life. It means you desire to please him above everything else. When your heart is focused on making his heart happy, you needn't follow a list of rules. He will keep your heart in line with his, and this will be your source of peace.

Which sounds more peaceful: attending an elaborate wedding, or planning every detail of it? Even those of us who love to be in charge would have to admit it is more relaxing to be a guest at a carefully planned event than it is to be responsible for it. How lovely of the Lord to have taken care of our lives, down to the smallest detail! It's up to us to accept all his careful planning. We can be "that guest" who smuggles her own food in and tries to persuade the DJ to play her party mix, or we can eat the beautiful meal prepared for us and then dance for joy no matter the song.

God, as I desire to walk in step with you, I am learning to trust your will. Help me to see your law as a path to peace. Keep me from stumbling as I go.

Those who love your instructions have great PEACE and do not stumble.

Psalm 119:165 NLT

A Good Struggle

My suffering was good for me,
for it taught me to pay attention to your decrees.

PSALM 119:71 NLT

When we're struggling or suffering, it's hard to imagine embracing a verse like this. *How could I ever see this situation as good for me?* We may even be tempted to think we'd rather stay the way we are, to know less of God's decrees. But we would be mistaken. There is a gift hidden in every struggle.

Take encouragement from the author of this verse. King David experienced repeated mortal danger, extreme discipline due to terrible choices, and a thorough humbling of his heart. If he could grow to appreciate the hardest times in his life, then we—with the Lord's help—will be able to do the same.

David said his suffering had been good for him; he was grateful for having been humbled. Just as it's hard to imagine being thankful for pain, it is also a challenge to fathom being glad for humiliation, demotion, or discipline. Yet, again, there is always blessing in the Lord's lessons! Facing our flaws invites us to acknowledge how much we need the Holy Spirit's help. Recognizing a weakness allows us to rely on the power of God. Realizing our sin opens the door to greater intimacy with our Father.

Father, I read these words, and I am filled with hope. To know that no matter what I face, you can use it to teach me, shape me, and make me better gives me courage. I won't pretend I enjoy suffering, but I do love knowing I can one day look back and see the gift you hid in the struggle.

Only Pray

Then he will pray to God, and He will accept him,
So that he may see His face with joy,
And He will restore His righteousness to that person.

JOB 33:26 NASB

We all long to be accepted. Some people are willing to go much further than others to gain acceptance, but we are all united in our desire to have it. Which material possessions or physical attributes will ensure we fit in? By worldly standards, the answer changes daily. By God's standards, though, the system is always the same: we pray to him, and he accepts us. No makeover or freshly renovated house is required. Just as we are, we are accepted. To the King of kings, we fit in.

Can you imagine if everyone you encountered found you utterly delightful? For most, such a favored time ended around the age of two. Yet, no baby is preoccupied with how to make people like them. These days, we tend to wonder if we're doing it right from the way we look, the actions we take, and the very words we speak. Who is it we're trying to impress? What makes their acceptance so important?

The only one worthy of such effort is the Lord, and, amazingly, he is the only one who doesn't place conditions on us becoming part of his "in" crowd. He restores, he welcomes, and he loves, while we need only pray.

God, when I think of the effort I've expended trying to be accepted here, I can only shake my head in bemusement. How beautiful it is to realize I need only speak your name to be welcomed by you. I pray, and you usher me in.

Show Me

The LORD said to Moses, "I will do the very thing you have asked, because I am pleased with you and I know you by name." Then Moses said, "Now show me your glory."

EXODUS 33:17-18 NIV

If a person you'd never exchanged more than a few words with asked to borrow your car, you'd most likely hesitate. If your best friend asked though, you'd hand the keys over in an instant. Intimacy welcomes openness. We love to do things for those we are closest to.

How intimate are you with the Lord? Would he be a little surprised to get a request from you, or do you talk so regularly that he already knows exactly what you need? How delighted will he be to show you his glory, to answer your prayer?

"Anything you want, anything at all, it's yours." Who hasn't fantasized about hearing something like that? What would we ask for? Depending on the day, our minds might jump to something simple like a good night's sleep, something practical like a fully paid mortgage, or something altruistic like an end to hunger.

Having pleased God, Moses chose to see God. Specifically, to see his glory. What an awesome request. Would you have thought of it? Yet, what could be better? What could possibly compare?

God, I want to delight you! Not simply to have my requests answered, but because I want you to know me by name. I want to be your friend. Will you show me your glory?

Uncountable Blessings

The LORD your God will bless you with full barns, and he will bless everything you do. He will bless the land he is giving you.

DEUTERONOMY 28:8 NCV

"Count your blessings" has become a cliché. It's one of those things we say without really even thinking about. But have you ever tried to actually do it? It only takes a few minutes to consider the people, experiences, opportunities, beauty, and second chances we've been given to realize it can't be easily done. We have been given too many blessings to count.

What kind of day might you have if you make a conscious effort to notice every good thing, thank God for giving it, and collect the blessings like tiny lights? How brightly would you glow by day's end?

You could be overwhelmed by the immeasurable lightness of God's goodness, or overwhelmed by routine and responsibility, forgetting your "blessing watch" before breakfast. Either way, ordinary blessings are always around to be counted. And sometimes there are extraordinary blessings to count as well. Try to count what likely cannot be counted: the innumerable ways God has blessed you.

God, every good thing is from you. I usually thank you for the obvious ones, but I know I often miss the little ones. Holy Spirit, help me recognize every element of goodness in this day. Overwhelm me with how blessed I am to be showered with good and perfect gifts.

He will bless EVERYTHING you do.

Let God Decide

This is the boldness we have in God's presence: that if we ask God for anything that agrees with what he wants, he hears us. If we know he hears us every time we ask him, we know we have what we ask from him.

1 JOHN 5:14-15 NCV

Think of a time you had to ask for something you really wanted. Maybe you wanted your parents to approve your first unsupervised trip, or perhaps you believed you were ready for more responsibility or more compensation at work. Your first goal was to get your parents—or your boss—to agree with you. However, this only works when what you ask for is what is in line with what they think is best. It is just this way with God. When we want what's in line with his purpose, we can ask boldly, assured of his yes. Because of his great love for us, we needn't be afraid to surrender our will to his.

A sixteen-year-old asking to go to Fort Lauderdale with a group of college students isn't likely to get an enthusiastic yes from her parents. No amount of reasoning will convince them the trip is in her best interest. They see a bigger picture due to their combined wisdom and experience. Though she may threaten never to speak to them again, they love her enough to say no. When she grows up, she'll likely be amused she even asked—and grateful they said no.

Let us remember we are like immature teenagers compared to God. Let us continually allow him to be like a good parent to us and to trust and obey when he says no.

Lord God, you know my motives, my needs, and my capabilities so much better than I do. I trust you to decide what's best.

Papa's Here

"As a mother comforts her child, so will I comfort you;
and you will be comforted over Jerusalem.
When you see this, your heart will rejoice
and you will flourish like grass."

Isaiah 66:13-14 NIV

Few images are more precious than a mother soothing her child. She holds the child close, gently swaying and whispering comforting words. "It's okay. Mama's here. I've got you." Through the prophet Isaiah, the Father promises his children that same loving comfort.

You will be comforted. You will rejoice and flourish. Papa's here. He's got you. All will be well. Believe it! No matter how things look today, settle into the sway. Listen to his words and be comforted.

Even if not today, a day will come when you are fighting tears. Guess what? There is no need to fight! Store this truth up for the day you need it, and the next time you find yourself holding back, holding it in, and barely hanging on... don't. On that day, go ahead and cry. Cry like a baby and let your Abba's comfort wrap around you as you hear his whispered words of comfort.

Abba Father, I love that I will never outgrow your arms. Your lap will always have a spot that fits me perfectly. Thank you for your loving comfort and for your promises of a joyful future.

A Wise Counselor

You will show me the path of life;
In Your presence is fullness of joy;
At Your right hand are pleasures forevermore.

PSALM 16:11 NKJV

It's not uncommon for young people to wonder what to do with their lives. Which college to attend. Is college the best fit? What career path to embark on. Which relationships are building us up, and which are holding us back? Whether from a guidance counselor, pastor, parent, or other trusted adult, wise advice from someone who cares helps guide the way.

As we get older, the world seems to expect us to figure things out for ourselves. What a blessing that as Christ-followers, we need never go it alone. The wisest, most wonderful counselor of all is living inside us, and he is always ready to put us on the right path.

One of the most precious gifts of life in the Spirit is the "continual revelation of resurrection life" mentioned in Psalm 16. We are guided daily in his Word and through constant nudges, impulses, and instincts. Go right instead of left, wait instead of run, call and check on that friend you can't stop thinking about. Whether we are aware at the time or not, we are constantly being rescued, blessed, and saved: each step bringing us ever closer to the Savior.

God, I know you want me to find the path to joy. Thank you for sending your Spirit to make sure I do! Thank you for not expecting me to have it all figured it out; instead, you send me a wise, wonderful counselor to show me the way.

In your presence is fullness of joy.

Psalm 16:11 NKJV

Sorrow into Dancing

You changed my sorrow into dancing.
You took away my clothes of sadness, and clothed me in happiness.
I will sing to you and not be silent.
Lord, my God, I will praise you forever.

Psalm 30:11-12 ncv

There's a beautiful moment during most funerals when, if you look around, you see everyone is smiling. The stories have begun to flow, and the laughter along with them. The quirks, habits, and renowned stories that made our loved one who they were bring us joy through the sadness. Happy memories ease the pain of loss. Love endures and changes sorrow into dancing. God designed it this way. He designed us this way. Whatever pain we feel, through his compassion, he turns to strength. The sadness we bear, through his love, can turn to joy.

Perhaps you have not yet reached the place where the joy of reminiscing outweighs the sadness of loss. If you have lost someone close to you or have suffered other trials, be sure to trust God with your heart and memories. In time, he will guide you through your mourning.

Know that it's okay to dance, to laugh, and to feel glad. Picture the one you loved waiting for you in heaven. Imagine them dancing for joy and clothed in gladness. Jesus wants you to feel that same happiness, even now as you live on earth. Give him your grief and sing his praises in exchange.

Father, your love is amazing. As I spiral into sadness, you take my hand and twirl me into joy. You transform grief to gladness as I remember the joy of what was.

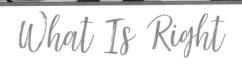

What Is Right

Make every effort to live in peace with everyone and to be holy; without holiness no one will see the Lord.

HEBREWS 12:14 NIV

Is there a peacemaker in your life? Perhaps you have a friend or relative who can't rest while others are at odds. It's likely they are always butting heads with those who can't let go of a grudge or agree to reconciliation. What is it that makes both the peacemakers and grudge-holders so passionate? Both have a strong conviction of what is right.

Sometimes when we feel we have been wronged, all we can focus on is assigning blame and standing our ground—that feels like the right thing to do. For peacemakers, what's right is peace regardless of fault or blame. According to Hebrews, we are likewise called to pursue peace this way. We are to love each other unconditionally, continually forgiving any wrongs. It is by becoming the peacemaker ourselves that we grow in holiness and see the Lord.

"Make every effort to live in peace... and to be holy." Lest we be tempted to think these are two separate instructions, let's notice they are contained in the same sentence. They are not mutually exclusive concepts; rather, one fosters the other. It's a process. One leads naturally to the other, and so we conclude: the path to holiness is peace. Why does this matter? Because the path to Jesus is holiness. If you want to run, you need to stand.

God, inspire me to pursue the peace that leads to where you are. I don't need to be right; I need to be with you.

Life and Light

You are the fountain of life,
the light by which we see.

PSALM 36:9 NLT

If lost in the desert, would you long for water or sand? Fumbling in the dark, would you search for light or squeeze your eyes shut? When thirsty, you crave water. In darkness, you seek light. Your body knows what you need. Spiritually, God is both your sustenance and the light that leads you to it. His truth is what nourishes you while his Spirit draws you in. His grace is your salvation. He is author and perfecter, beginning and end, supplier and supply.

God is the standard bearer. His beauty helps us recognize beauty. His truth reveals truth. His light is how we know light. This is the opposite of the world. Here, light is easier to pinpoint in darkness, beauty is more obvious against a backdrop of dreariness, a fountain is more prized in a parched land.

God's light is incomparably, incomprehensibly bright. His life flows like a fountain that never runs dry. Without him, true refreshment and light simply wouldn't be; they cannot exist outside of him.

God, you set me up so I cannot fail to find you! You designed me to thirst, and because you love me, you became living water. You created me to seek light, and then made yourself the brightest star in the sky. Thank you, God, for being both light and life.

Lift You Higher

I call to you from the ends of the earth when I am afraid.
Carry me away to a high mountain.

Psalm 61:2 NCV

Have you ever walked through a maze? Even if you can easily navigate one on paper, it's quite a different experience without a bird's eye perspective. In the thick of it, all you can see is the hedge directly in front of you. Having no other choice, you take it one turn at a time. Inevitably, without that overhead view, you'll make a wrong decision. You may even get lost, repeatedly coming up to the same dead end.

When life feels like that maze, call out to God. Follow his voice to the next turn and the one after that. Allow his hand to lift you up—higher than your own sight—and show you the way through.

We can call out to the Father for direction and perspective. We can also call to him when we need to be rescued. Rather than sink into fear, huddled in a corner of the maze in defeat, we can pray. No matter how far we've travelled, God will hear us. His loving hand can pluck us straight out of our fear and set us on the mountaintop of his promises. Our circumstances may not change right away, but our hearts will lighten immediately. In that high, safe place with him, troubles fall away.

Father God, you are always listening and waiting to guide me. You see whether I am headed the right or wrong way. What a comfort it is to know I can call to you and follow the sound of your voice. I can extend my arms and you will lift me up, showing me more than I can see on my own.

Better than Life

Because Your favor is better than life,
My lips will praise You.

PSALM 63:3 NASB

"That dress is to die for! Where did you get it?" We have all heard or used such hyperbolic expressions before. While we don't really mean we would dive off a mountain to own the perfect dress, we use the phrase "to die for" to indicate how great we think something is. Perhaps we use it to describe a delectable dessert or diamond earrings. It's so delicious or appealing we say we would trade our life for it.

Only one thing is truly to die for, and that's life with the Father. Do you believe that on a perfect day what God has prepared for you is so much better that you'd gladly give it all up? It's hard to fathom, isn't it? Yet that's what his Word tells us. God's love for us is unimaginably good—better than even the most wonderful earthly objects and experiences.

How intimately the Psalmist must have been connected to God to write these beautiful words: to think that a sweet touch from the Lord, a whispered forgiveness, or a tender reprieve was the greatest treasure in his life. This is the type of intimacy the Lord wants with all of us. How awesome is that?

Father, your love is hard to fathom. Blessings here are but a taste of the blessings in heaven. Love here is only a kiss of the love there. Beauty here is only a glimpse of what is to come. Life here can be good, but you are better than this life! Praise you, God, for your unimaginable goodness.

PSALM 63:3 NASB

BECAUSE YOUR FAVOR IS BETTER THAN LIFE, MY LIPS WILL PRAISE YOU.

Seek Him First

Fill us with your love every morning.
Then we will sing and rejoice all our lives.

PSALM 90:14 NCV

Seek him first. Why are we encouraged both in the Word and by our fellow believers to begin our days with the Lord? If you already begin your mornings with him, you know what a perfect start to the day it is.

Settling into his Word first thing creates an awareness of his nearness, a desire to remain close to him, and an overflowing of his love. We see through his eyes, rendering everything beautiful. We feel with his heart, making everyone lovable. We move with his purpose, giving meaning to our every action. With God's Spirit so near, what else can we do but sing for joy?

Good news and bad news. Which do you prefer to hear first? Most of us choose the bad news, so we can get it over with. We want to deal with the negative, then move on to happier matters. By pleading early for mercy, we can turn our attention to praise, rejoicing, and gladness of life with God. By handing him our burdens first thing, we are free when it's time to dance. Seek him first each day, and joy will follow.

Precious God, make my day! Show, move, and lead me in your way. Fill me with compassion, purpose, and awe. Allow your overflow to touch everyone I encounter so that their day will be made better.

FILL US WITH YOUR LOVE EVERY MORNING. THEN WE WILL SING AND REJOICE ALL OUR LIVES.

PSALM 90:14 NCV

Lying in Dust

I lie in the dust;
revive me by your word.

PSALM 119:25 NLT

How does this verse sit with you? Your response can tell you about the current condition of your heart. Were you pierced with feeling for the writer or for those you know who are lying in the dust? If your heart responded with compassion, it is a sign your soul is feeling strong. If this surprises you, take heart, you are doing better than you realized.

If, when you read this, you felt as though you could have written it, then you are laid low. Take care not to let the ground claim you. It will try. Reach up your hand. Grab onto God's and let him revive you. Cling to the promises in his Word: promises of better days, rejoicing, healing, mercy, and grace. Hold on and feel your spirit rise.

Perhaps it's been one of those days. Wearily, you wave your white flag and lie down. "I'm done," you declare. "I give up." It may seem like the best place to be, but you're vulnerable when lying low. The enemy doesn't respect the white flag. As you curl up in defeat, he layers on sadness. On the guilt, he piles up shame. But God offers a solution. Contained in the pages of Scripture is more hope, encouragement, healing, and promise than you can imagine. The next time you find yourself curled up in defeat, rise up from the dust and be revived by the power of God's Word.

Savior, I need only cry out, and your hand of mercy will begin to lift me. I need only remain in your grasp, and your restoration will be mine.

Choices that Build

The wisest of women builds her house,
but folly with her own hands tears it down.
Proverbs 14:1 esv

If you were to see a mother bird ripping her nest apart, how would you feel? Confused? Concerned? A mother dog refusing her hungry puppies tugs similarly at our hearts. It's unnatural. Now imagine a woman too busy to make it to volleyball, too harried to pack lunches, or too overwhelmed to accept an invitation to coffee. It's not as hard to picture, is it?

Twig by twig, we have the option to build our homes—our relationships, our lives—or to destroy them. Every "harmless" complaint about a husband, every forgotten birthday of a friend, every time sleep is more important than a morning hug goodbye, the nest is weakened. Keeping close to our Lord, he leads us to the choices that build, sustain, and strengthen our homes.

"If I knew then what I know now…" Who hasn't thought or said these words before? If only wisdom were innate! Instead, it seems we often get wise by making—or witnessing—foolish mistakes. If only gentle warnings were enough to make us steer clear of choices that weaken our foundation. If we lean into God's Word and trust his wise, perfect plan for our lives, bad decisions will happen less frequently, and we will grow wiser with each one.

Dear God, remind me today of what is important. Help me to be a builder: to reinforce the structures of connectedness, affection, and respect that make my house strong. Make me wise, Father, and make me strong.

Hear My Prayer

"If my people, who are called by my name, will humble themselves and pray and seek my face and turn from their wicked ways, then I will hear from heaven, and I will forgive their sin and will heal their land."

2 Chronicles 7:14 NIV

Cause-and-effect might be the earliest concept we grasp. A baby cries, and someone comes to soothe her. A toddler sees different results when he asks nicely or throws a tantrum. We sometimes approach prayer from this simple mindset. If I cry out to God, he'll come running. If I ask nicely, he'll give me what I want. However, that's not how prayer works.

If we want to be heard, we need to come humbly, quietly, and seek God's face. The first step is simply to be in his presence. We must regret that which distances us from him. We need to reject our sins and ask for forgiveness. Then we can await his response.

How extraordinary to be called by the name of God. We are children of the King, beloved of the Savior, and family in Christ. As the Church, we are even his bride. When we joined his family, he gave us his name. What confidence this inspires. What hope! He will always hear our prayers and, surely, as we come humbly before him, there is nothing he won't do for us.

Father, forgive me for the times I approach you like an infant, wailing my needs without first acknowledging your greatness. Forgive the sins I cling to and fail to confess. Hear my prayer, God, offered in love and reverence, and silence my cries.

Keeping Watch

He will not let you stumble;
the one who watches over you will not slumber.

Psalm 121:3 NLT

What is the longest you've ever gone without sleep? Most of us have at least one all-nighter in our memory. Chances are, you collapsed into sleep at the first opportunity afterward. No matter how important our assignment, or how vital our vigil, we all eventually need to stop and sleep.

God is the exception. The one who watches over you and makes sure you won't stumble as you navigate today's rocky terrain, never stops watching. While you work, sleep, struggle, and settle, the Lord keeps watch. If this is true, where was God when a loved one died, a child became addicted, or someone betrayed you? It can be tempting to dismiss a verse like this when it doesn't reflect our experience. What are we to make of these lofty promises?

It might feel like this verse was written for others. When your life is filled with stumbling, you have to believe the Lord sees it all. He's keeping careful guard over your eternal soul, and he will not let you go. He sees your suffering, but he's preparing a place for you with him where every second of pain will be forgotten. He's got you.

God, you never take your eyes off me. How can this be? Each step I take is of concern to you. You won't let me fall. You refuse to lose me. With each wrong turn, you guide me back to the right path. Every hour I sleep, you watch over me and replenish my strength. Thank you for your constant presence.

You Are His

You are a chosen people, royal priests, a holy nation, a people for God's own possession. You were chosen to tell about the wonderful acts of God, who called you out of darkness into his wonderful light.

1 PETER 2:9 NCV

Did you know God chose you for life in the family of Christ? It's the most wonderful invitation in all of history, and it was extended to you. He knew just when and how to reach out to you: he planned it from the moment he dreamed you up. Had he not ordained it, your heart would have remained closed to him.

Maybe he gave you a longing for more meaning in your life and then led you into Christian community. Perhaps he allowed you to hit rock-bottom, to need a radical life change, and then he lifted you out of the depths. Regardless of how it happened, he chose you. He called you by name and made you his.

Athletes make great coaches and ex-addicts make wise treatment counselors because they have learned from personal experience. We learn best from someone who has been where we are. They relate better. Just as God may have used someone else's story to reach you, he wants your story to reach someone else. He lifted you out of the darkness because he wanted to be with you but also so you could tell others about life in the light.

God, I'm continually amazed that you chose me. You imagined me, made me, and let my life unfold in such a way that I would end up choosing you back. Reaching into the darkness, you took hold of my heart and lifted me into light, love, and hope. Today and forever, I am gratefully yours.

Worthy of Glory

Give unto the Lᴏʀᴅ the glory due to His name;
worship the Lᴏʀᴅ in the beauty of holiness.

Psᴀʟᴍ 29:2 ɴᴋᴊᴠ

Imagine walking into your home and noticing a gift on the counter with your name on it. It's not your birthday, or a holiday, or an otherwise special time in your life. *What's the occasion?* you wonder. *I was just thinking about you* is written on the card attached. It feels wonderful to be appreciated just for being you.

As lovely as it is to receive such surprises, we should enjoy giving them even more. Do you surprise the people you love with gifts, notes, or hugs to let them know you love them simply for being who they are? More importantly, when was the last time you praised God just for being God? He loves to receive spontaneous gifts of honor and praise just as much as we do, and he is far worthier of such glory.

What are some of your favorite names of God? There are so many to choose from: King of Kings, Lord of Lords, Prince of Peace, Jehovah, Wonderful Counselor, Comforter, Savior, Father, I Am. Each name deserves such glory and honor. Can we ever do them justice? What of his beauty, grace, holiness, and majesty? We could sing forever and never come to the end of the ways he is worthy of our praise.

God, above all other names, I worship yours. I contemplate your holiness and perfection, and I realize I can never thank you or worship you enough. I love you for who you are, and I thank you for who you are making me to be.

Open My Understanding

Then he opened their minds to understand the Scriptures.

Luke 24:45 esv

Can you remember enjoying a book or film as a child, then revisiting it as an adult? How amazed were you to discover all you'd missed? It's like discovering the old, familiar painting in Grandma's attic is a masterpiece by a renowned artist. Our adult minds understand more of the humor, recognize layers of context, and interpret subtext in a way we couldn't as children.

When it comes to understanding Scripture, we are all children. Different aspects of Christ's character are revealed as we grow and mature in our faith. God chooses when and how to enlighten us, so like that favorite childhood story or movie, every return to a Bible passage can hold fresh revelation.

What an awesome moment it must have been for the disciples. After grieving Jesus' death and fearing for their own lives, he had appeared among them, invited them to examine his wounds, and even sat down to share a meal with them. At once, the veil of understanding was lifted, and everything he had ever said made sense. They finally understood what he had done and what they would begin to do. Jesus wants to open your understanding so you can comprehend the Scriptures too.

Lord God, open my mind to the incredible, living truth of your Word. Every day show me more of who you are and who you would like me to be. Thank you for your Word and for making it eternally new.

Room for Humility

"He must become greater and greater,
and I must become less and less."

JOHN 3:30 NLT

Imagine you are famous. Everywhere you go you are followed. Every time you speak you are listened to. Every choice you make is emulated. You are loved, admired, and respected. Now imagine willingly walking away, leaving the spotlight, and silencing your influence. It doesn't sound easy, does it? If it doesn't sound easy in the context of a daydream, how much harder must it be in reality? We are naturally inclined to want approval and love attention.

Humility is hard. It's not natural, yet it's a requirement of a life centered in Christ. The words of John 3:30 were spoken by John the Baptist, one of the humblest people in the Bible. He knew when he met Jesus it was time for a prophecy to be fulfilled. As brightly as his light had shone, and as meaningful as his work had been, it was time to direct the light—and people's attention—toward Jesus.

A full garage can't hold another car. A full glass can't contain any more liquid. If we want to bring in more, we must first make room. If we want God to take over and guide our lives, we must first surrender our own plans. If we desire his will, we must let go of ours.

Father, help me to be humble. Let me take the example of one far greater than I and turn any admiration I receive onto you. When people look at me, may they see you. When I am heard, let the words be yours. If I am followed, let it be on my way to you.

Prize Beyond Value

To the one who works, his wages are not counted as a gift but as his due. And to the one who does not work but believes in him who justifies the ungodly, his faith is counted as righteousness.

ROMANS 4: 4-5 ESV

Even if you have your dream job and every day is a pinch-me-so-I-know-I'm-not-dreaming day, you'd probably stop working if your employer decided they would no longer pay you. Conversely, if you acted as though your paycheck was an entitlement regardless of job performance or attendance, you'd undoubtedly be fired. Both employee and employer have a responsibility to do their part.

This is how it works in the job market, but it's not how it works with Jesus. In order to earn our wages of eternal salvation, all we have to do is believe in him. That's it. No work, no rules, and no sacrifice. He's already done it all. It's far from fair, and yet our just God willingly offers it.

Sometimes companies will give away a dream prize as a way of generating excitement and attracting new customers. The spectacular vacation, or shiny new car, or years' worth of free product can't be purchased or earned. Hopeful winners must submit their entry and wait. God dreamed up the first and best sweepstakes ever. The prize is beyond value. No amount of money or effort could purchase it. Hopeful winners must submit their entry and... everyone wins! The prize too valuable to put a price tag on is free to anyone who asks for it.

Jesus, I will never stop being amazed by your selflessness. You did all the work and made all the sacrifices. Thank you for the unearned gift of my salvation.

Wanted and Chosen

God decided in advance to adopt us into his own family by bringing us to himself through Jesus Christ. This is what he wanted to do, and it gave him great pleasure.

EPHESIANS 1:5 NLT

Adopted children have the privilege of going through life knowing they were wanted by their adoptive family. They don't have to wonder if they are in their family by mistake: their very presence in the home is proof they were chosen. What a comfort and a blessing, to know you are wanted and chosen.

This same blessing is afforded to you as a child of God. He chose and adopted you specifically because it pleased him to do so. He didn't bring you into his family to save the world, or to end all war, or for any other grand purpose. He simply wanted you.

Perhaps you know a couple who spent months or years dreaming of and praying for a child to adopt. You would have witnessed an incomparable anticipation as they awaited this child's arrival. Afterward, their joy must have been equally incomparable. Imagine God's delight as he planned out the adoption of each and every one of his beloved children. Imagine the explosion of joy and sound of angels' voices singing in anticipation of our arrival! How beautiful it must have been, and must still be, as he waits for each of his own to come to him.

Oh Father, I'm so grateful you chose me, though I confess sometimes I can't imagine why. I focus on my failures and flaws, and I'm tempted to think of how disappointed you must be. But you're not. You love and accept me as I am.

Safe in His Arms

He will cover you with his feathers, and under his wings you can hide.
His truth will be your shield and protection.

Psalm 91:4 NCV

Like an eagle protecting its young, God shelters us under his mighty wings from every storm and attack. No pelting rain or arrows can touch us. This picture is both powerful and tender. How safe and secure we are, and how peaceful it is to be nestled in against his warmth.

Do you rest in God's protection, or do you struggle like a young bird, eager to leave the nest and fly? Are you constantly poking your head out, trying to get a peek at the action? Maybe you've even slid out from underneath those sheltering feathers, and now you're flying alone, vulnerable to enemies and elements. If you are, fly home. Nestle in.

Beyond the physical picture of God's protection, of his mighty wings and strong arms, we have also the safety of his truth. If he said it, we can stand on it. We are on the side of majesty, of beauty, of anything that is good; we are also on the side of his protection.

God, you are my shield and my protector. Thank you for providing me such a safe place to wait out the storms and hide from the attacks this world hurls my way. Forgive me for the times I leap from your protection, thinking I don't need shelter. I will always need you.

Respond in Peace

If it is possible, as far as it depends on you,
live at peace with everyone.

ROMANS 12:18 NIV

Does living in peace with everyone you know sound possible? Paul clearly didn't know anyone like the people you have to deal with. Maybe you find this easy because harmonious relationships are all you know.

Most of us land somewhere between these two extremes. We find people are generally easy to get along with, except that one co-worker, moody child, or rude cashier. Sometimes living at peace with everyone can seem like an impossible dream. Look at the phrase tucked into the middle of the sentence, *as far as it depends on you*. We can't do anything about the way people behave toward us, but we do have a choice in we respond. Calling on the Holy Spirit's help, we can always choose to respond in peace.

Why do you suppose Paul prefaced his encouragement to peaceful living with two caveats? Perhaps it's because he knew that peace is the ideal we aim for even if it can't always be the reality. The first condition is *if possible*. It may not be. There may be relationships that cannot, no matter what you do, be harmonious. It's okay to accept this. The second qualification is *so far as it depends on you*. Once you've done all you can, you may need to wait for the other party to do the same. While you wait, be at peace.

Holy Spirit, hear my prayer. To every slight, slur, and disagreement, may I respond in peace. Through my peaceful responses, may others see your goodness and grace.

Not Yours to Know

Just as you cannot understand the path of the wind or the mystery of a tiny baby growing in its mother's womb, so you cannot understand the activity of God, who does all things.

ECCLESIASTES 11:5 NLT

Imagine a toddler who has just wrapped her mind around the meaning and power of what is surely the most wonderful little word in all of language. "Why?" She will use this word to try and understand everything that comes across her path: bedtime, grandma's wrinkles, the food on her plate, the blue sky, and babies inside mommies. *Why? Why? Why?*

With maturity, we learn to stop verbally questioning everything we come across. However, this innate curiosity remains because we were made to wonder. Often our questions can be answered. Yet, when it comes to God's own mind and the decisions he makes, the answers are not ours to know.

Is your phone nearby? Hold it in your hand for a moment. Test its weight, turn it around, and look at every angle. How does it do all it does? It's incredible, isn't it? Most of us are quite content with not having the first clue how it works, we are simply glad it does. May we feel the same about the incomprehensible, marvelous mind of God.

Father, I long to know you! There are so many whys I'd love you to answer. Help me wait. Help me rest in your sovereignty and learn to embrace those things about which I can only wonder.

Intimate Companion

"God is spirit, and those who worship him
must worship in spirit and truth."
JOHN 4:24 ESV

How do you define *spirit*? An athlete triumphing over great hardship is said to have an indomitable spirit. A feisty, strong-willed child is sometimes described as spirited. What's being described in both cases is something beyond the body, something intangible.

Though equally intangible, we are able to interact with the Holy Spirit. He works in our lives by teaching, comforting, and protecting us. His promptings tell us when to move closer and when to pull back. The Spirit is our intimate companion, and wholly deserving of our worship.

There are those with whom we share a bond that defies all the laws of time and space. It's as if when we first saw them our hearts said, *There you are! I've been waiting for you.* Our souls recognized what our minds had not yet time to grasp: we are connected. This is the worship—the connection—the Lord wants from us. Beyond Bible studies, stirring sermons, and fervent prayers, he wants to connect with our souls. He wants to be our most intimate companion.

Holy Spirit of God, I doubt I realize even a fraction of the ways you influence and guide the course of my life, and yet I can't imagine life without you. How can I express enough gratitude? How can I show enough love? Though I know it will never be enough, I give you all the worship I can.

High Standard

God's truth stands firm like a foundation stone with this inscription: "The Lord knows those who are his," and "All who belong to the Lord must turn away from evil."

2 Timothy 2:19 NLT

When a rule is firm and unchanging, we say it is written in stone. Between parents and children, most of these rules are about keeping everyone safe and healthy. Almost uncannily, a parent seems to know when one of these hard-set rules is being, or has been, broken. They know their children so well that something feels off.

Our Father knows us even better than earthly parents can know their children. He also commands us to turn from sin. These two truths form the foundation of our faith. We are known, and we are called to a high standard. He loves us and wants us to be safe. When we stray, he sends conviction followed by grace to turn us back to him.

Participation trophies are not prized possessions. The awards and accomplishments we cherish are the ones not easily obtained. It might seem daunting to try to meet God's expectations. You might feel like you can't do any better than a participation trophy when it comes to always doing the right thing. Remember that God knows you. He is aware of the weaknesses you have, and he offers you his grace.

Wise Father, thank you for knowing me and being my firm foundation. I could say I wish it were easier to break your rules and not get caught, but it wouldn't be true. I'm so grateful you love me enough to want to keep me in your grace!

What Is Right

The fruit of that righteousness will be peace;
its effect will be quietness and confidence forever.

ISAIAH 32:17 NIV

Righteousness. What a powerful word. Perhaps you have shied away from it in the past. The term can conjure up images of rigidity and unattainable perfection, especially if you have known someone who was overly self-righteous. If you look closer, though, what is promised here when you pursue righteousness is peace, quietness, and confidence. It sounds lovely, doesn't it?

A righteous life is one that puts the Lord first by seeking to honor him in what you say and do. When you love what is right, you are honored with the gift of peace. Your life is quiet because there is no discord. You are confident because you know you have nothing to be ashamed of.

Can it really be this simple? Can choosing "right" really bring on peace? Can the result of a life lived for truth and fairness really be quietness and trust? Surrendering the struggle of getting your own way certainly sounds peaceful. Taking the road of harmony certainly seems quiet. Why not try and see?

Father, I want to live righteously. Help me ask before every decision if what I am choosing is right. Make love of truth and goodness such a part of me that with time I won't even need to ask because I will know. And knowing, I will act, speak, love, and live with righteousness.

The fruit of
that righteousness
will be peace;
its effect will be
quietness and
confidence forever.

Isaiah 32:17 NIV

One True God

Since the beginning of the world
men have not heard nor perceived by the ear,
Nor has the eye seen any God besides You,
who acts for the one who waits for Him.

ISAIAH 64:4 NKJV

Authenticity matters. We crave it. It's important to us that the gemstone, the handbag, or the promise is real. We want to know if we can trust people and if they are telling the truth. If we have been let down or lied to, we will scrutinize situations in the future to be sure of authenticity.

What a comfort it is to worship the one true God! We needn't scrutinize. We don't have to ask. All his promises are true. All his gifts are good. His love is authentic, and it is ours.

The Bible contains many mentions of lower-case gods. Our culture is filled with them as well. Since the beginning, people have sought out and made-up substitutes. Those of us who know the one true God are puzzled by these false, lesser gods. Why would anyone want a created deity over the Creator? No made-up god exists purely to love and be loved the way our God does. What more could we possibly want, and where can we imagine ever finding it?

Almighty God, you are the one and only God. I trust you, I love you, and I believe you. How is it that you care for me and actively participate in even the tiniest details of my life? May my worship reflect my awe; may it be authentic.